Adaptation and Survival

Richard Spilsbury

WAYLAND

First published in 2015 by Wayland

Copyright © Wayland 2015

All rights reserved.
Dewey number: 578.4-dc22
ISBN 978 0 7502 9640 3
10 9 8 7 6 5 4 3 2 1

Produced for Wayland by Calcium

Editors: Sarah Eason and Leon Gray
Editor for Wayland: Julia Adams
Designer: Paul Myerscough
Illustrator: Geoff Ward
Picture researcher: Maria Joannou
Consultant: Michael Scott OBE

Printed in China

Cover photograph: Shutterstock/iDesign.
Interior photographs: Dreamstime: Holger Leyrer 18, Outdoorsman 9, 11; FLPA: Mark Moffett/Minden Pictures 33, D P Wilson 16; Fotolia: Fabrice Beauchene 10, 45, Reisbegeleider.com 23, Warren Rosenberg 29; Istockphoto: Alexander Laws 41, Gaspare Messina 32, Dra Schwartz 20, Vickie Sichau 25t; Photolibrary: Animals Animals/Breck P Kent 38, Marevision 17t, Michael S Nolan 36; Science Photo Library: Eye of Science 21t; Shutterstock: Alle 19, Tatiana Belova 15, Riaan van den Berg 7, Qing Ding 43, EcoPrint 17b, Flashon Studio 37, iDesign 31, Peter Ingvorsen 30, Eric Isselée 5, 26, Cathy Keifer 6, Chai Kian Shin 25b, Kevin H Knuth 35, David Mckee 3, 28, Mike Norton 12, Seleznev Oleg 13, Tyler Olson 27, Lee Prince 22, Silver-John 34, Dwight Smith 14, Victor Soares 4, 40, Stubblefield Photography 21b; Richard Spilsbury: 24.

Wayland is an imprint of Hachette Children's Group
Part of Hodder & Stoughton
Carmelite House
50 Victoria Embankment
London EC4Y 0DZ

An Hachette UK company   www.hachette.co.uk   www.hachettechildrens.co.uk

SAFETY NOTE: The activities in this book are intended for children. However, we recommend adult supervision at all times as neither the Publisher nor the author can be held responsible for any injury.

Contents

CHAPTER 1

What is adaptation?

An adaptation is a physical feature or behaviour that helps a living thing survive. Adaptations allow animals and plants to be successful in their habitat. To be successful, animals and plants need to be healthy so they can reproduce and contribute to the survival of their species.

Different adaptations

Physical adaptations are body features or structures that help an animal, plant or any other living organism get food, keep safe, have shelter, withstand bad weather and breed. One example of a physical adaptation is the shape of a bird's beak, which helps it get the particular food that it eats. The two parts of the crossbill's beak cross either to the left or the right. This enables the bird to prise open the tightly closed scales on tree cones and extract the seeds from within them to eat.

Behavioural adaptations are the ways living things act to help them survive. For example, people adapt to the cold by putting on warm clothes or staying in heated houses. Other types of behaviour include animal calls and migration. Whales make different calls or sounds to locate or identify each other in the oceans. Many whales also migrate vast distances every year from summer feeding waters to winter breeding waters.

The chameleon's tongue is perfectly adapted to catch fast-moving insect prey. The tongue is about as long as its body. It can be rolled out incredibly quickly, and it has a sticky suction cup on the end.

Owls have huge eyes. In fact, if human eyes were proportionally the same size as an owl's, they would be the size of grapefruits! Owl eyes are large to absorb all the available light when they fly at night. This adaptation helps them find prey and to look out for predators in low light.

Evolution of adaptation

Adaptations are the result of evolution. Evolution is a change in a species over a long period of time. It happens because individuals in a species are all slightly different. Within a species of hunting mammal, for example, some individuals will be born with longer, sharper teeth and the ability to run faster than others. These features help them catch prey more easily, so they are healthier and live longer. When they reproduce, their offspring will also have longer, sharper teeth and will run fast. Over time, the individuals that are not so well adapted to their habitat may die out. Eventually, all members of the species will share the long, sharp teeth and fast running adaptations. This process is called natural selection and takes different lengths of time for different species – usually hundreds to tens of thousands of years.

CONVERGENCE

Organisms that live in different parts of the world, but within similar types of habitats, often have similar adaptations. This is called convergence and occurs when adaptations prove the most successful solution to the challenges of living in a particular habitat. For example, most burrowing animals generally have small or no eyes because eyesight is redundant in the darkness deep underground. They also all have different enhanced senses, such as smell or touch, to find their way around. Many burrowers have a streamlined shape and small limbs to help them burrow. The European mole, golden mole of Africa and marsupial mole of Australia are not related, but all have convergent adaptations that have helped them survive in similar environments.

Habitats

A habitat is the type of area in which an organism lives. For example, squirrels live in forests and fish live in water. Habitats offer resources to organisms and support living processes.

The most important resources are light, oxygen, temperature, water, nutrients and space. Plants use sunlight, air and water for photosynthesis. This is a process by which plants make food. Plants take in carbon dioxide from the air through their leaves and water from the soil through their roots. They use the energy found in sunlight to convert the carbon dioxide and water from the soil into sugars, providing plants with food.

Frogs require water in their habitat so they can lay eggs and so the tadpoles that develop from the eggs can grow into frogs.

The entire community of living things, and the habitat in which they live and interact, forms a complex network that is known as an ecosystem.

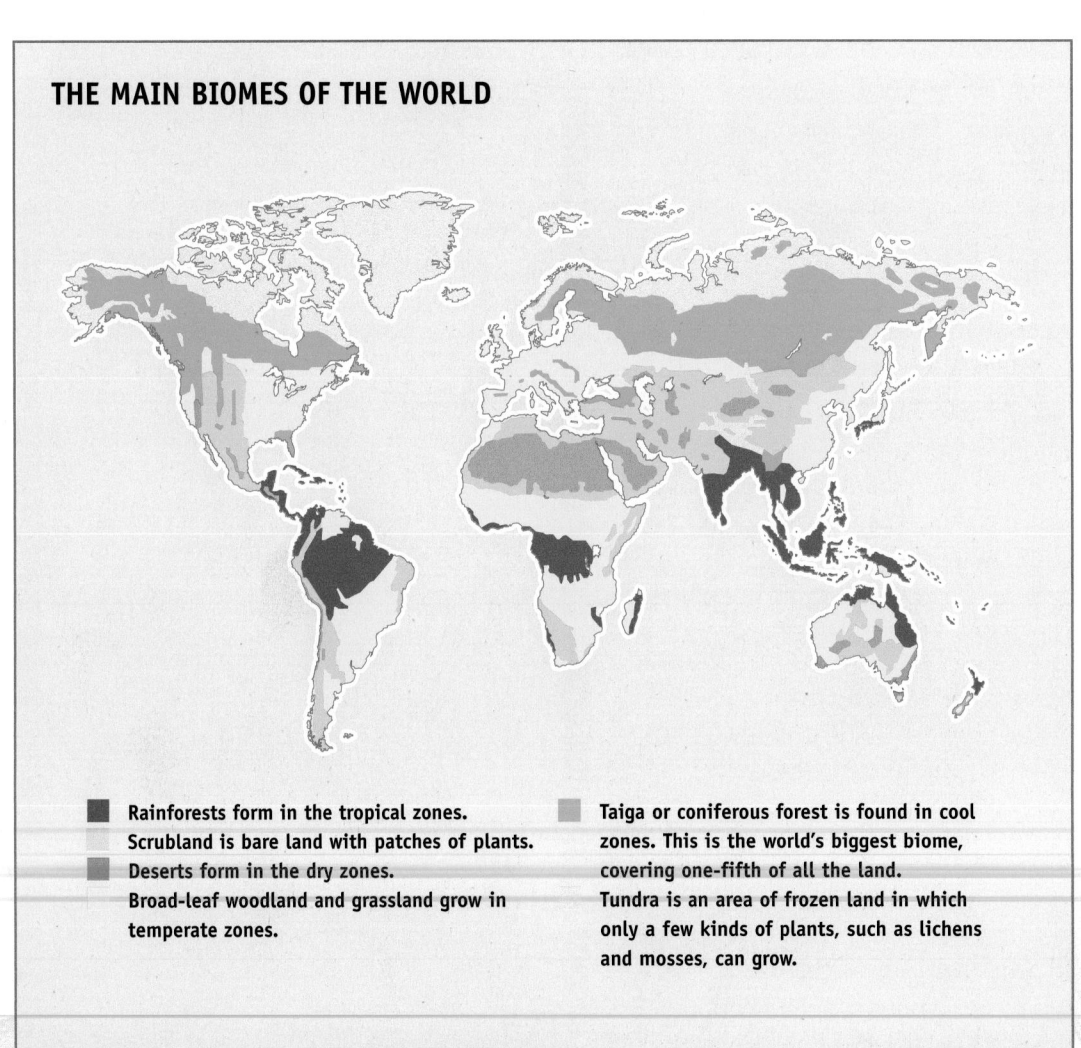

THE MAIN BIOMES OF THE WORLD

Rainforests form in the tropical zones.
Scrubland is bare land with patches of plants.
Deserts form in the dry zones.
Broad-leaf woodland and grassland grow in temperate zones.

Taiga or coniferous forest is found in cool zones. This is the world's biggest biome, covering one-fifth of all the land.
Tundra is an area of frozen land in which only a few kinds of plants, such as lichens and mosses, can grow.

Biomes

A biome is a distinctive group of ecosystems that covers a large area of Earth's surface. Deserts, rainforests and polar regions are examples of biomes. Particular plants and animals live in particular biomes because they are adapted to the conditions there. In northerly parts of Russia, northern Europe and Canada, for example, where cold, snowy dry conditions persist for most of the year and summers are short, the biome is taiga forest. Many of the animals adapted for life in the taiga, such as bears, ermine and moose, have thick fur to keep them warm.

The polar bear is a key species adapted to tundra, with thick, white fur for warmth and camouflage when hunting seals.

BIOME CLIMATES

The world's biomes differ mainly because of their climates. Climate is the long-term average of the weather conditions that occur in a particular location. Some climates are hot and wet, while others are cool and dry. You only find certain animals and plants in a particular biome because they are adapted to live in one type of climate.

Habitat demands

Each biome has its own particular combination of climate, living things and availability of resources, such as food or water. Animals and plants that live in a particular biome have developed a range of adaptations to survive there.

Extreme cold

The coldest places on Earth are the polar regions and high mountain-tops. Life is hard because the temperatures are extremely cold, there are strong winds, and all the water is frozen as ice. Freezing temperatures can damage the tissues of an organism's body severely and slow down living processes until the animal or plant shuts down and dies.

Few plants can survive in these harsh conditions. Some, such as the arctic willow, survive by growing very low to the ground to avoid the icy winds. The alpine snowbell flowers in spring. Buried beneath snow, dark buds absorb sunlight and gradually melt the snow around them so the flowers can open in the air.

The dominant plants in the taiga are conifers such as fir, pine and spruce. They have long, needle-like leaves that are covered in a thin layer of wax. This protects the leaves from damage by the freezing temperatures, and it also stops them from drying out. The narrow shape of the leaves means there is less surface area through which water can evaporate. The shape of the trees allows snow to slip off easily without breaking the branches.

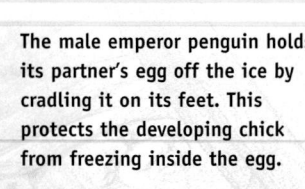

The male emperor penguin holds its partner's egg off the ice by cradling it on its feet. This protects the developing chick from freezing inside the egg.

Polar animal adaptations

Warm-blooded animals, such as the polar bear, maintain constant body temperatures no matter how cold the surroundings. These animals have natural insulation to stay warm – a thick fur coat and a layer of fatty blubber under the skin. A bird called the rock ptarmigan shows a behavioural adaptation to keep warm. It makes a burrow under the snow, and the snowy shelter keeps the bird warm. Antarctic cod make a protein in blood that works like antifreeze, preventing their bodies from freezing in the icy Antarctic waters.

The layer of blubber beneath the skin of a walrus may be up to 10 centimetres thick.

INVESTIGATE:
Blubber insulation

YOU WILL NEED:
packet of lard, 2 plastic bags, large bowl, ice cubes, water

Investigate how blubber insulates some mammals that live in polar regions. Cover one hand with a plastic bag. Put a generous amount of lard into another plastic bag. Put the plastic-covered hand into the middle of the lard-filled bag. Tape the bag tightly at the wrist to seal the bag. Cover your other hand with two plastic bags. Place each hand in a bowl of ice water. Record the temperature of the water, and time how long each hand stays in. Ask your friends to try the experiment. Draw a table like the one below and record the results. They should show that the hand covered in lard (to represent the blubber of mammals that live in polar regions) can stay in the icy water for longer.

Researcher	Plastic bag hand, time in water	Blubber hand, time in water	Notes

Desert heat

Deserts are hostile environments. The intense daytime heat can dehydrate and burn, while the night-time temperatures can be very cold. It rarely rains in the desert, and when it does it pours. The challenges for desert-dwelling animals and plants are to find and keep as much water as possible and survive the intense heat.

Plants of the desert

Cacti are perfectly adapted to desert life. Their roots grow far and wide just below the surface to collect dew or a few drops of rainwater. Many cacti have large, grooved stems, which expand to store any surplus water. As the water is gradually used up, they shrink again. Cactus leaves are long, thin needles. This reduces loss of water by evaporation and acts as a barrier to animals that might steal the water. Cactus stems are green because they contain the chlorophyll. This pigment traps the energy in sunlight so the cactus can make food.

Many desert plants are annuals. After a burst of rain, their seeds germinate quickly. The plants grow, flower and die, all in a short time. The annual releases seeds before it dies. The seeds have tough, waterproof coats that resist drying, so they can survive underground until the next rains come – perhaps several years later.

Saguaro cacti grow in the deserts of south-western United States and Mexico. The roots of these plants can grow up to 15 metres long. The roots do not reach deep into the ground, but rather stretch out around the plant to reach underground water sources.

Animal adaptations

There are few large desert-dwelling animals. Small mammals escape the heat of the desert sun by sheltering in the shade of plants or burrowing underground. Many are nocturnal, which means they are active during the night and rest during the day. Others radiate body heat to stay cool, for example a jack rabbit has huge ears, covered with blood vessels. When blood circulates through the ears, body heat is given off. This helps to keep the animal cool.

Some desert-dwelling animals have various adaptations to get water and keep it. Many seed eaters, such as the kangaroo rats, make water by breaking down the fats in seeds. Snakes retain water by excreting solid uric acid rather than liquid urine. Few desert animals have sweat glands to avoid losing too much water in sweat.

LIFE ON SAND

It is difficult to move and live on the hot desert sands. Many desert-dwelling plants have widely spreading roots to anchor them in the shifting ground. Some animals, such as camels, have broad feet to stop them from sinking in to the sand when they walk. A snake called the sidewinder slips quickly across the sand in a sideways S-shaped movement so that its body hardly touches the sand.

The camel's hump does not contain water. It stores fat, which insulates the camel's insides from the desert heat.

Ocean survival

There are countless living creatures in the world's oceans. All of them are adapted to life in the water. In the salty seawater, one major problem is getting enough freshwater. Many marine animals, such as fish, drink the salty water and then excrete the salt through their gills. Others, such as seals and whales, get the water they need from the animals they eat.

Ocean light

Marine organisms also have to adapt to get enough light in the murky ocean depths. Plant-like seaweeds need the energy from sunlight for photosynthesis. The fronds of many seaweeds contain air sacs that help them float near the surface where there is more light. Seaweeds found in deeper waters are often red rather than green. The blue wavelengths of sunlight penetrate deeper into the water, and the seaweed's red pigment is better at absorbing these wavelengths. Seaweed does not grow below about 20 metres because very little sunlight penetrates to that depth. In deeper, darker water, animals such as comb jellies and cuttlefish create their own light through bioluminescence. Chemical reactions inside the bodies of these animals create light patterns that help them locate prey or mates.

Breathing underwater

Marine animals have two methods of getting the oxygen they need. Fish and other animals that live permanently under the water breathe oxygen in the water, either through their gills or skin.

A jellyfish has a circular bell at the top of its body, which helps it float, and hanging tentacles that sting and capture food to eat.

Other marine animals breathe oxygen from the air at the surface of the ocean and store it in their blood and muscles to keep them going when they dive.

Water pressure

Some animals that dive deep underwater, such as whales, have lungs and rib cages that collapse to cope with huge water pressure. If this did not happen, the ribs would break and pierce the lungs. Many fish have swim bladders – sacs of gas inside their bodies – to counteract water pressure and make them buoyant. Some animals, such as cuttlefish, take water into their bodies and then force it out to help them move.

The tuna's body colours are adapted for defence. The blue upper body disguises it from predators swimming above. The white underside disguises it from predators below as they look up towards the sunlight.

INVESTIGATE:
Fish tails and other traits

Investigate how the different shapes of tails and fins and the position or shape of eyes and mouth on a shark, goldfish, flounder and eel are adapted to their different niches. You can do this by studying them in an aquarium or zoo or by looking at books or the Internet. Present findings in a chart like this.

Fish	Body part	Adaptation	Purpose	Habitat
Flounder	Eyes	Both on the same side of head	To allow clear vision from the seabed	Seabed

Life on the edge

Coasts lie at the edges of the land and sea. The organisms that live there have to cope with twice-daily tides that submerge them under salty water or leave them exposed to the sun, wind and predators. They also face the force of the waves, which can knock them from their habitats or against hard rocks.

The large, claw-shaped holdfasts of this kelp are exposed when the tide is out. When the tide comes in again, the holdfasts will fix the kelp onto the rock.

Shore adaptations

Many coastal animals and plants have adaptations to cling tightly to rocks so they are not washed away by the tides. Instead of roots, seaweeds have holdfasts that do exactly as their name suggests. Finger-like projections anchor the seaweed to the rock. Seaweeds also produce slime that keeps them moist when the tide is low.

Marine invertebrates called mussels have threads that protrude out of their shells and attach to rocks. Limpets have large, broad feet that act like a suction cup and suck the shell tightly to the rock. The limpet clings onto the rock so tightly that even the roughest wave cannot knock it off.

Hard shells are physical adaptations to protect the animals inside. A crab's shell protects it from knocks and also camouflages the animal against the background of sand and rock to keep it safe from predators. Like many other coastal animals, the crab can also escape heavy seas or the drying sun by burrowing into the sand.

Mussels do not move to find food. They feed by drawing water through one opening in their shells, filtering out edible particles, and then forcing the filtered water out through a different opening.

LIMPET ROUTES

Limpets move like any other animals. They extend their muscular feet and move slowly on the surface of rocks in search of algae. Limpets can travel up to a metre from their home spot, leaving trails that show where they have been. Since they always return to the same spot, limpets create small depressions, called limpet scars, in the rock on which they live.

The soft and fleshy body of a crab is protected from predators by the hard, tough shell that surrounds it.

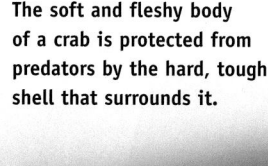

Diving beetles breathe air through tiny holes in their abdomen. At the surface of a pond, they push their abdomen into the air and collect air bubbles. When they dive underwater, the beetles breathe from the air bubbles.

Freshwater challenges

Freshwater habitats, such as lakes, rivers, and wetlands, present organisms with other challenges. Steep mountain rivers have fast-moving water that can wash organisms away from the places where they live and feed. Some wetlands, such as estuaries, contain freshwater for part of the time but fill with saltwater when the tide comes in. In some wetlands, the water fills with silt, which makes it difficult for animals to see.

Adaptations for moving water

River animals have various adaptations to stay in one place in the fast-flowing water. Some, such as water snails, suck onto surfaces. The stonefly nymph grips the edge of the rock with its claws.

The caddis fly larva builds a protective coat of gravel around its body that holds it firm. Streamlined shapes also allow water to run smoothly over an animal's body. This makes it less easy for the water to wash them away.

Some river plants have leaves adapted to avoid damage by the rushing water. Floating bur reed has long, thin leaves that reduce resistance to water flow. The leaves drift in the direction of the water current, rather than trying to stand upright and taking the full force of the flow. Water milfoil has feathery leaves through which water easily flows.

Estuary adaptations

Plants such as glasswort store fresh water in their fleshy stems or leaves so they can survive in the salty water of marshes and estuaries. Others, such as cord grass, have special filters on their roots to remove salt from the water it absorbs. Freshwater also contains more oxygen than saltwater. Tidal changes therefore change the amount of dissolved gases in the water. Mangrove trees on muddy tropical shores have roots that grow from halfway up the trunk. The root tips burrow underground, but the upper parts stay above water. Special pores in these parts of the roots absorb oxygen from the air to supply the waterlogged roots below.

A coat of gravel protects the caddis fly larva from predators. It also anchors the larva to prevent it being swept away by water.

INVESTIGATE:
Echolocation

Animals such as river dolphins use echolocation in the deep, murky water of their freshwater and ocean habitats. They give off high-pitched sounds and then listen for the echoes that bounce off nearby surfaces. This information tells them where and how far away their prey or an obstacle is. Try it for yourself. Ask a friend to blindfold you and then clap once from ten different positions around you. You should note down where you think they were each time they clapped. Then swap and repeat the exercise. How many times were you each correct and what affected how well you both did?

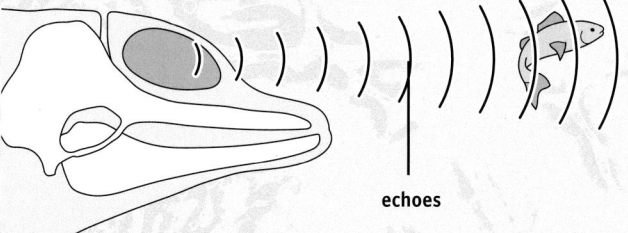

echoes

In the air

The ability to fly or glide to find food, shelter or a mate and to escape danger requires special adaptations such as wings. Animals need to create more lift than their weight to fly. However, moving through the air is not restricted to animals – plants also have adaptations to help them spread seeds through the air so they can grow in new places.

Aerial adaptations

Most flowering plants spread their seeds so the seedlings do not have to compete with their parents for resources such as space and light. Some plants, such as poppies and orchids, produce tiny, lightweight seeds that drift for kilometres in the wind. Some, including

ash trees, produce seed containers shaped like wings that enable them to twist away on a breeze. Maple seeds grow in pairs. Wing-like blades spin like tiny helicopters, carrying the seeds long distances. Dandelion and thistle seeds are attached to a thin stalk topped with wispy threads. These act like parachutes and can be carried by gentle breezes.

Flying animals

Insects and birds are the main flying animals. They have strong muscles in their chests, or thoraxes, to flap their wings up and down. Pushing the wing against the air below produces lift. Some animals, such as beetles and geese, have bigger muscles in relation to their bodies but also wider wings to create more lift. The feathers on the wings of a bird are adaptations to increase the surface area of wings with low weight. The shape of muscles and feathers creates a wing with a curved cross section – similar to the wing of an aeroplane – that provides lift as the bird flies forward.

Flying squirrels do not fly – they leap and glide between the treetops. A muscular flap of skin grows between their front and back legs on both sides to help them glide through the air.

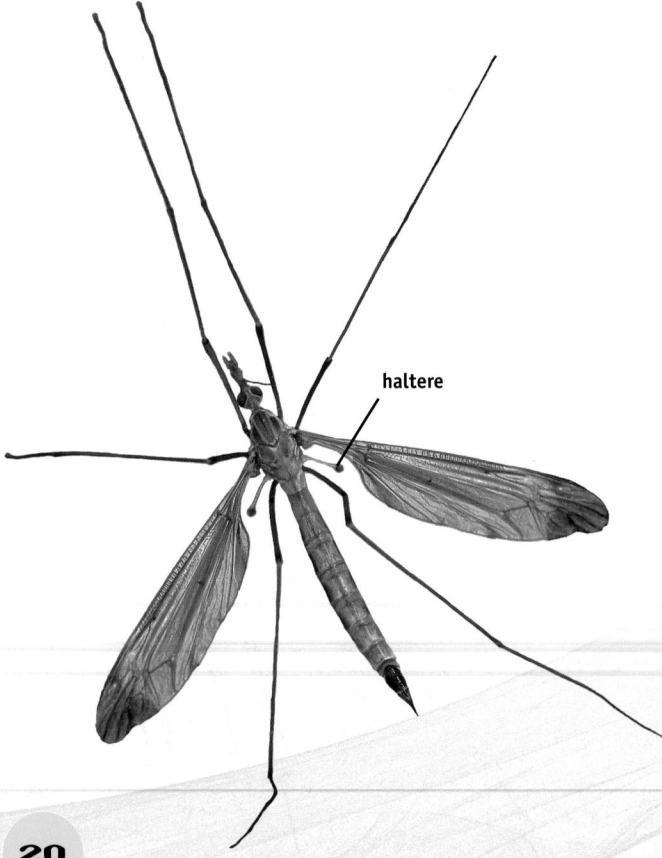

haltere

Behind each of a crane fly's wings is a haltere. These small, golf-club-shaped structures are adapted from what was once a second pair of wings. In flight, the halteres vibrate rapidly. They help the flies keep balance when flying.

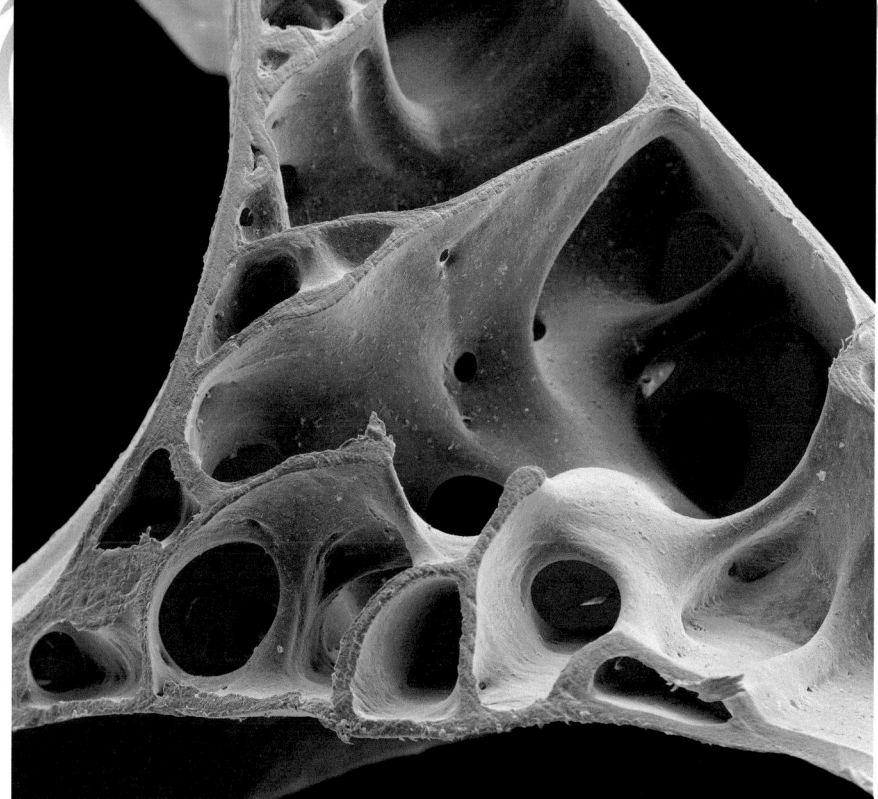

Bird bones are adapted to help them fly. To make them lighter, many birds have hollow bones. These have struts or bars inside them to keep them strong. This photograph shows the interior of a falcon's bone.

Bats are the only mammals that can truly fly. They have wings of stretched-out skin between long, finger-like bones. Bats move the thin, wide surfaces of their wings in a sort of rowing motion to fly through the air.

Some birds such as puffins have stubby wings that are better for 'flying' underwater and are not very good at flying in the air.

BIRD WINGS

The shape of a bird's wings is adapted to its style of flight. Eagles and vultures have long, wide wings with spread feathers that catch rising warm air to help them glide while they search for food on the ground. Birds with shorter wings, such as blackbirds and grouse, can take off quickly to avoid predators but cannot glide well. Fast-flying birds such as swifts have narrow, curved wings to reduce air resistance and produce more forward thrust as they hunt insects on the wing.

Interactions

The community of plants and animals in an ecosystem interact with the habitat around them. Interactions are the way things act upon or affect each other, for example, the way animals compete with each other for food or plants compete for space to grow. Organisms coexist by adapting to cope with, and benefit from, these interactions.

Competing for resources

All organisms compete for resources. Individuals of the same species compete with others, for example, for the best areas to live. Species also compete with others for resources, such as food and shelter.

In shady woodland, light is one of the biggest challenges for plants. Different plant species have different adaptations to compete for light. Trees and shrubs grow taller to reach the sunlight. Brambles and other climbing plants twine around trees to reach up to the light above. Epiphytes such as ferns can grow from the highest branches to reach light.

The strangler fig has an unusual adaptation to compete for precious light in the rainforest. It starts life as a seed in the top of a tree. The roots grow down to the forest floor by wrapping tightly around the host tree.

Starved of light and food, the host of a strangler fig eventually dies and the strangler fig tree's roots unite to form a hollow trunk.

INVESTIGATE:
How woodland plants compete for light

Survey a section of woodland to find out what adaptations plants have to capture sunlight. Don't try to survey the whole woodland. Measure out an area of about 10 square metres. Count the number of different species that have a particular type of adaptation there and draw a bar chart to show your results. Along the y-axis (horizontal) you could label the columns with the different adaptations (growing tall, climbing plants, epiphytes, and clearing plants). On the x-axis (vertical) you should have the number of plants you find in each category.

The strangler fig tree's leaves grow above the host tree and starve it of light, and the roots take all the available water and nutrients.

Sharing resources

Organisms also coexist by adapting in ways that allow them to share available resources. They adapt to their own particular ecological niche so that they can share, rather than directly compete, for a resource. For example, eagles and owls feed on rodents and small birds and often hunt in the same woodland habitats. Eagles are diurnal birds of prey, which means they hunt during the day. Owls are nocturnal predators, which means they hunt at night. So the two never directly compete for the same food source. Whales coexist in the same habitat because they feed in different depths of the ocean. Humpback whales feed on krill near the surface of the oceans, while grey whales dive to the sea floor to feed on small crustaceans such as crabs.

Vultures and lions feed on the same types of animals. Lions catch and eat the fresh prey, while vultures are scavengers and eat the leftovers.

Hunters

Carnivores have many special physical adaptations to compete for food with other members of the same species. The great white shark is an apex (top) predator. It hunts fast-moving prey such as sea lions. To locate prey it has special senses in its snout that detect the tiny electrical currents produced by sea lions and other prey when they move. The shark also has an acute sense of smell that can detect a drop of blood in the water up to 5 kilometres away. It has razor sharp, serrated (jagged) teeth to grab and tear flesh. The teeth are continually replaced when worn down.

Cobras have sharp, hollow fangs that squirt poisonous venom into their prey to kill it.

Some predators have camouflage colours to sneak up on unsuspecting prey. Tigers have dark stripes on a pale background, which breaks up their outline as they stalk through the forest and tall grass of their habitat.

Hunting behaviour

Hunters also have behavioural adaptations to catch prey. Some predators, such as lions and wild dogs, hunt in packs to bring down large or fast animals they could not catch alone. Chimps use sticks to dip into tree holes to get ants. Sea otters use stones to crack open mussels and other bivalves.

This spider's camouflage is both a physical and behavioural adaptation. Its colour camouflages it against certain flowers in its surroundings. The spider finds a similarly coloured flower, sits and waits, and then pounces on flies that land there.

CARNIVOROUS PLANTS

In some habitats, such as swamps and marshes, the soil is nutrient poor. Carnivorous plants survive in these places by feeding on animals. Marsh pitchers have jug-shaped leaves that contain scented digestive juices. Insects are attracted to the smell and fall inside the pitcher. The pitcher plant then slowly absorbs the insects. Bladderworts are aquatic plants. They suck aquatic larvae into air-filled traps through special trap doors. The plants then digest the trapped prey.

The wide open leaves of the Venus flytrap have short, sensitive hairs. When an insect touches the hairs, the leaves snap shut. The insect is trapped inside, where digestive juices dissolve it.

The larva of an insect called an ant lion sets a trap to catch its prey. It burrows backwards into sandy soil to create crater-like pits. The larva waits at the bottom of the pit with its wide jaws sticking up. When ants or other small insects pass by, the ant-lion larva flicks sand at them until they fall into the pit. After sucking them dry, the larva throws them out of the pit and waits for its next meal.

Once an insect falls into the pitcher plant, it can rarely climb the plant's slippery walls to escape.

Animal defences

Just as hunters have adaptations to catch prey, prey animals have adaptations to defend themselves or hide from danger. Some animals have physical defences, such as tough protective coverings. Tortoises tuck their heads and legs into their hard shells, hedgehogs roll up to form a ball of sharp spikes, and the scaly anteater, or pangolin, is covered with overlapping, horny scales. When threatened, the pangolin curls up so the scales cover the body like a coat of armour.

Other animals use camouflage. Some insects look like sticks or leaves, moths have patterns and colours that resemble tree bark, and speckled flatfish are almost invisible as they lie on the sandy seafloor. When the giant swallowtail caterpillar sits still, the brown and white blotches on its body make it look like a large bird dropping.

Some animals have bold markings and bright colours on their bodies, which act as a warning to predators that they may be dangerous.

The colours of this yellow-banded poison dart frog advertise that it is poisonous if bitten, so predators leave it well alone.

MIMICRY

Some animals have adaptations to mimic other animals, often as a form of defence. Many poisonous animals have bold, bright colours to warn predators that they are dangerous. The harmless Sinaloan milk snake has red and yellow rings that are almost identical to the highly poisonous coral snake from the same area. As a result, snake-eating birds do not eat either species. For the same reason, some non-poisonous South American tree frogs mimic poisonous frogs from the same areas.

Animals also have behavioural defences. Rattlesnakes shake the rattle on the end of their tails to warn animals that they are dangerous. Many animals make themselves look bigger and behave aggressively to startle would-be attackers. For example, some toads stretch out their legs, inflate their lungs with air and tilt their heads down.

Plant defences

Some plants have physical defences to deter animals from eating them. Think of the thorns on a rose plant or the spikes on a bramble. Others have chemical defences. The stem of the euphorbia contains poisonous sap to deter or even kill plant eaters. Stinging nettle leaves are covered with tiny hairs containing poison that break at the slightest touch. The broken edge of the hair cuts the skin of the animal that touched it and letting poison into the wound.

Other plants have defences to protect them from cold or bad weather. Some plants protect their delicate flowers from cold or wet weather by closing their petals. The petals of crocuses open up in warm weather but close when it gets colder. Daisies fold up their petals before it rains.

Many animals stay away from stinging nettles so they do not get stung by their defences.

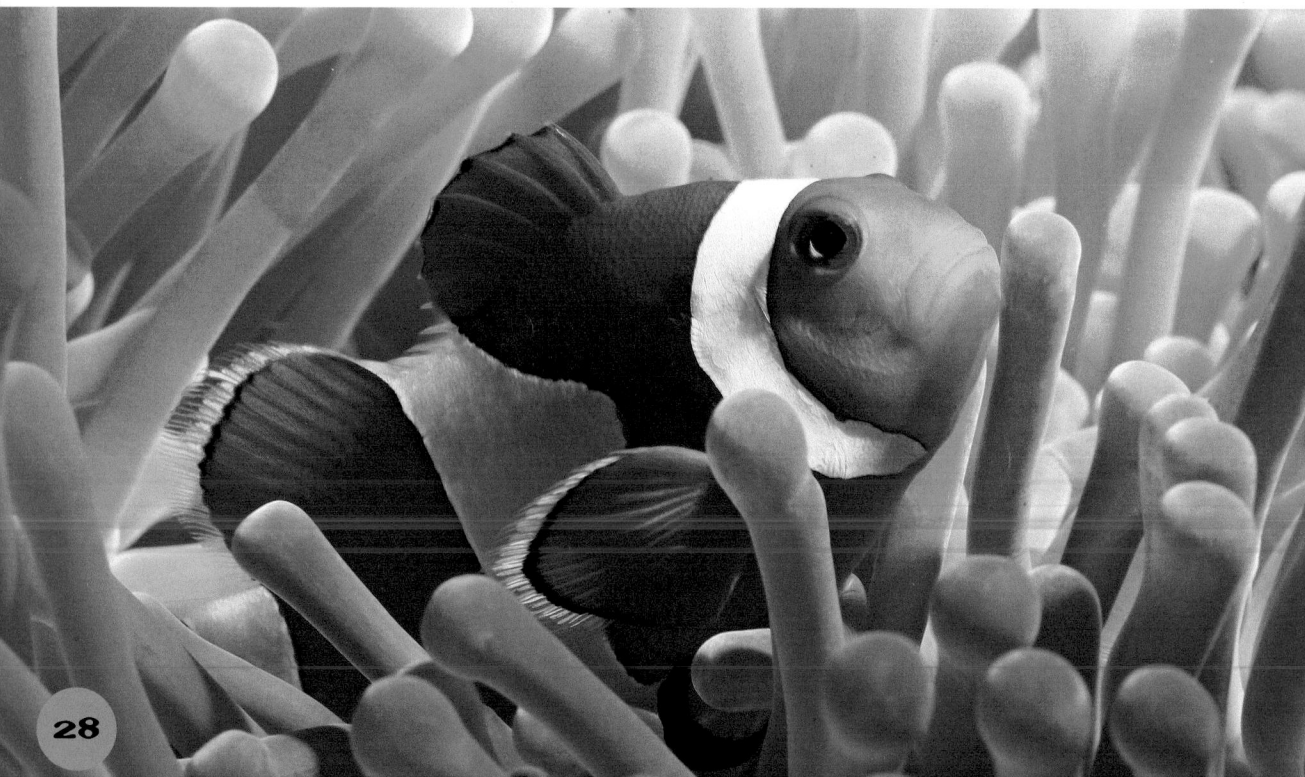

CHAPTER 4

Social interactions

Some adaptations are linked to social interactions between organisms. For example, they may bring animals together in the same habitat to breed. There are also adaptations that plants have to encourage insects to pollinate their flowers. This is an example of co-evolution.

Helping each other

Some adaptations allow organisms to live together so that both benefit from the relationship. This is called symbiosis. One example of symbiosis is the relationship between trees and fungi. More than 90 per cent of all trees have fungi growing in their roots. Fungi help trees absorb nutrients and water.

In return, the fungi get food, such as sugars and amino acids, from trees. Another example of symbiosis is the feeding relationship between the honey

The sea anemone has poisonous tentacles, but the clownfish is immune to the stings. It lives safely among the tentacles, out of the reach of predators. The anemone benefits because the clownfish chases off butterfly fish that would otherwise feed on it.

badger and a bird called a honeyguide. The honeyguide calls loudly after finding a bee's nest. This attracts the attention of the honey badger and leads it to the nest. The badger tears open the nest to eat the wax, honey and bee larvae inside. The honeyguide is not strong enough to open the nest by itself, but it can eat the badger's leftovers.

Harming others

Parasites are organisms that live in or on other organisms, called hosts, and take food from them. The host gains nothing from the relationship. Indeed, the parasite may harm, or even kill, it. Parasites have special adaptations to allow them to live in or on their hosts. Tapeworms have hooks to hold on to the stomach lining of their hosts as they feed on the stomach contents. They have ribbon-shaped bodies that curl into the folds and tubes that make up the host's digestive system. Their outer layer is tough to avoid being digested

Head lice are tiny, wingless insects that are people parasites. The claws of the lice are adapted to grip onto hairs, and their mouthparts suck tiny amounts of blood for food.

by the strong digestive juices in the stomach. Fleas and lice use claws on their legs to hook into their host's skin as they feed on its blood.

ANT SYMBIOSIS

Ants have many relationships with other animals and plants. Ants and aphids have a symbiotic relationship. Ants protect aphid eggs during the winter and the aphid larvae as they feed on plant leaves. In return, the ants get a supply of honeydew, which is a sweet substance the aphids excrete. Bullshorn ants and acacia trees also enjoy a symbiotic relationship. The acacia has large hollow thorns that shelter the ants. The acacia's leaf tips are also a source of food for the ants. In return, the ants' wasp-like stings deter mammals that might eat parts of the tree. The ants also patrol the leaves and remove caterpillars that feed on them.

Reproduction

Animals have an amazing array of adaptations to help them find a mate. Some compete to attract mates with a colourful courtship display. A complex chemical reaction in a light organ on the underside of the female glow-worm's body creates a vivid green glow. The bright glow quickly attracts a male, which is just as well because the glow-worms live only for a very short time and have to mate and lay eggs before they die. Luna moths use scent to attract mates. Females release their scent at night. The first male to find a female will mate with her. As a result, the male moths have developed enormous antennae to detect the scent from afar.

Male peacocks have enormous, colourful feathers to attract attention. They display these to entice females (peahens) to mate and to warn off other males.

Some reproductive adaptations help males defend their territories. Red deer have large antlers to rut, or fight, with other males during the breeding season. Female frogs choose a male that has the best spot for laying eggs. The males call to attract the females and chase away rival males. The males use stretchy skin pouches in their throats to make their loud calls. These inflate and resonate to make the call louder.

INVESTIGATE:
Dissect a flower

YOU WILL NEED:
flower, sharp knife

Find a clear diagram of the male (stamen) and female (carpel) parts of a flower in a book or on the Internet. Take some flowers and use a sharp, fine knife to slice them open very carefully. See if you can identify the parts used in pollination and some of the adaptations to attract pollinators – such as colours, patterns, scent, and the shapes of the flowers. You could make a chart to compare the different flowers of different plants and their adaptations.

Pollination

Some plants attract animals to carry their pollen grains from the male parts of flowers to the female parts of flowers in other plants, where they can form seeds. Many plants have bright, colourful petals, scented nectar and particular flower shapes to attract different kinds of insects, birds or even bats to their flowers. For example, foxglove flowers are bright pink and shaped like tubes. Insects are attracted to a store of sweet nectar in the centre of the flower. The insects rub against the pollen as they crawl into the flower to feed. They carry this pollen to the next foxglove, where it rubs off on the female part of the flower.

Some plants have long floral tubes that hummingbirds pollinate. Hummingbirds hover next to the plant and dip their long beaks inside to reach the nectar. They pick up the pollen at the same time.

Group living

Many animals of the same species live in groups or colonies for mutual benefit. When threatened, a herd of zebra run and their stripes all blend together. This makes it difficult for predators, such as lions, to pick out a weak individual and allows most, if not all, of the herd to escape. Rodents called prairie dogs are vulnerable when grazing on open grassy plains. So one acts as a lookout while the others feed. The lookout makes different calls, depending on what predator it spots, to tell the others to returns to the safety of their burrows.

Some animals live in groups to share the care of their young. One of the reasons elephants live in herds is because the females help each other look after their young. Lionesses have a similar number of young at the same time, so all the mothers in the pride can raise them in crèches. This increases a cub's chances of survival because the lionesses can protect them against aggressive male lions.

Different roles

Social insects take on different roles in colonies to help them thrive. There are three types of ants in an ant colony: males, queens and workers. Each type

One meerkat acts as a sentry while the rest of the group dig in the sand in search of food. The sentry stands upright on the lookout for hawk predators, ready to call out at the first sign of danger.

queen

workers

These worker ants are caring for the queen ant and the eggs and larvae she produces for the colony.

of ant has a specific job to do. Males mate with the queen. The workers are divided into different groups to look after the queen and care for and guard the nest. Worker ants are specially adapted to their different roles. For example, some have large heads and jaws so they can defend the nest against attackers.

In gorilla groups, the leader is usually the biggest silverback male. He decides when and where to feed, rest and sleep and solves arguments between family members. The others have a subordinate role within the group and defer to the silverback's rule. In return, the silverback will risk his life to protect the group, for example, from rival silverbacks.

SPREADING THE WORD

Social insects communicate in different ways. Ants feed, lick and touch each other to share secretions that are chemical messages, telling each other what jobs need to be done in the nest. When a wasp stings, its venom contains a scent called a pheromone that warns other wasps of possible danger. This makes the wasps more aggressive. Bees use a visual form of communication – a figure-of-eight 'dance' – to tell other bees about the location, amount and quality of nectar nearby.

Changing environments

Organisms adapted to the conditions in a particular environment have another challenge to face: change. Environments change daily and seasonally and also over longer timescales. How do organisms adapt to these changes?

Day and night

Light and temperature vary throughout the day, and different animals and plants respond by adapting to the changes. During the night, many plants close their flowers and tiny holes, called stomata, on their leaves. Closing the flowers protects the delicate reproductive parts from the cold night air. Stomata are used to absorb carbon dioxide in the air, which the plant needs for photosynthesis. Since this cannot take place in the darkness of night, the stomata close to prevent the plant from losing valuable water.

Some animals respond to changing temperatures by escaping underground, so they have narrow body shapes and claws adapted for tunnelling. Arctic hares retreat to burrows during blizzards. Shore birds such as knots flatten themselves down in dips in the shingle when it is very windy.

The stems of these daisies have turned to face the sun so their leaves get maximum light. The stems adjust their position to track the sun as it moves across the sky each day.

Reptiles are cold-blooded, which means they get their heat from the sun. When it is cold, reptiles are slow and would be easy prey for their predators. If the reptiles cannot control their temperature by moving to warmer sites to warm up (or cooler sites to avoid overheating), they may change colour to vary the rate of heat absorption or heat loss. They get darker to absorb more heat and lighter to absorb less heat.

Marine iguanas bask in sunlight to increase their body temperature, which is reduced by the cold water in which they feed.

INVESTIGATE:
Leaves and light

YOU WILL NEED:
2 small pots, compost, radish seedlings, 2 cardboard boxes

Green plants harness the energy from the sun using a pigment called chlorophyll. They grow towards the brightest source of sunlight and also spread their leaves to expose the maximum surface area to the light. This response is called phototropism.

To test phototropism, germinate some radish seedlings in two small pots. When the seedlings are about 2 to 3 centimetres tall, put each pot inside a dark box with one side open. Put the two boxes near separate bright light sources, such as a small window, with the open sides of the boxes facing the light source. After a couple of days, you will notice that the seedlings have stopped growing upwards and bent their leaves towards the open sides of the boxes where there is most light.

Shifting seasons

Some parts of the world have distinct seasons with different weather patterns within each season. Many temperate biomes have hot summers with long days and cool winters with short days. Some animals move away to cope with the changing seasons, but organisms that stay put must adapt to survive the changing temperature, light, moisture and availability of food. The most obvious example in plants is the loss of leaves in deciduous trees such as oaks. Frost would damage the broad, flat deciduous leaves, so the trees simply shed the leaves and stop growing during the winter. They survive winter using the food stored in their roots.

The Arctic hare's white winter coat helps keep it warm and camouflages the animal in the snow. In summer, the snow melts and the hare moults, growing a grey-brown summer coat. The timing of the moult depends on the number of daylight hours.

Seasonal animal adaptations

Animals have different physical and behavioural adaptations to survive the changing seasons. Squirrels cache (hide) nuts and seeds in preparation for the lean winter months. Fish may move to the bottom of lakes and ponds because the temperature is warmer there than at the top, which may freeze over.

Deciduous trees rest in winter. At the end of the summer, the leaves turn from green to orange, red and yellow and brown, before dropping from the tree.

ALL CHANGE

Leaves contain different pigments, but the dominant green chlorophyll usually hides the other colours. As the days get colder, shorter and darker in the autumn, broad-leaf trees such as birch and elm produce less chlorophyll in their leaves. Eventually chlorophyll production stops, leaving a range of different coloured pigments. Without photosynthesis taking place, the leaves die and fall to the ground.

Many animals eat more in the autumn to fatten up for the winter. The fatty layer acts as insulation, and they can also use the fat as a source of energy if food is scarce. A beaver's sharp claws and teeth help it cut tree trunks to dam up small rivers and streams. The deep pond this creates provides the beaver with food, protection from predators and shelter in the winter. White-tailed deer produce different digestive enzymes in the winter so they can the digest different kinds of plant foods that are available at that time of year.

Staying put

Organisms can stay put when times are hard by becoming dormant. This means the animal or plant temporarily suspends growth, activity and development. Dormancy uses up far less energy during times when there are fewer available resources. Hibernation is common in mammals such as chipmunks, hedgehogs and mice. Hibernation occurs when cold winter weather stimulates a special, controlled drop in the metabolic activity of these animals. Mammals such as bears do not hibernate but enter a deep sleep from which they can wake for short periods to drink. Other animals change their body chemistry to survive the cold. For example, the blood of the wood frog is 100 times more sugary than human blood so it does not freeze during winter.

Aestivation is a hot weather equivalent of hibernation. It is found in snails, some frogs, and even fish. African and South American lungfish burrow into the mud at the bottom of ponds that are starting to disappear as the hot season approaches. The lungfish surround themselves in a mucus cocoon to save water, and they slow their metabolism to a fraction of the normal rate until the rainy season arrives again.

Moving on

Other animals avoid harsh conditions by moving to different places for part of the year. This is called migration, and it is common in some birds, turtles, fish, mammals and insects.

Animals that hibernate, such as this dormouse, usually cache food and prepare a sheltered resting place before they become dormant.

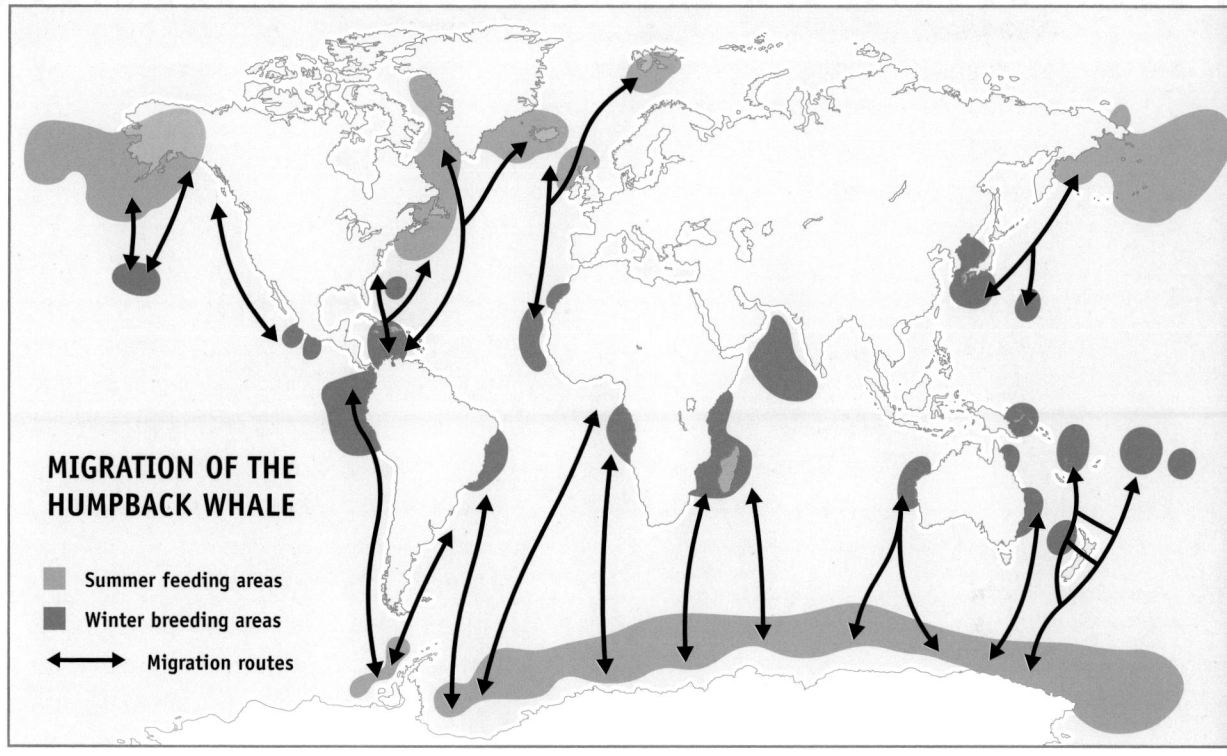

MIGRATION OF THE HUMPBACK WHALE

■ Summer feeding areas

■ Winter breeding areas

◄——► Migration routes

Humpback whales spend part of the year feeding in polar or Antarctic waters. They migrate to warmer oceans to breed.

Many geese and waders breed and feed their young in the long summer days on the tundra or mountains and move south (or north from Antarctica) to spend milder winters in temperate areas. The Arctic tern travels 22,000 kilometres from pole to pole in its migration. Other animals migrate much shorter distances. For example, toads move down the Alpine mountain slopes when it gets too cold at the top. Ladybirds may simply move inside buildings to escape the cold outside!

FOLLOWING THE ROUTE

Animals have different adaptations to migrate in the right directions. Some animals have in-built compasses! Sea turtles migrate long distances to lay their eggs on the beaches on which they were born. The brains of the turtles can detect Earth's varying magnetic fields, allowing them to navigate across the oceans. European eels breed in the Sargasso Sea off Bermuda. Their eggs hatch into tiny larvae that swim back to the rivers where their parents once lived in Europe. Eels make the long journey by using their highly developed sense of taste, which can detect differences in the saltiness of the water.

Rates of adaptation

Some environmental changes are slow and gradual. Most places on Earth have experienced 'ice ages' every 100,000 years or so. During an ice age, the climate cools down to freezing point for thousands of years and then slowly warms up again. Some species gradually adapt to natural changes like this, but others become extinct, which means they die out. Woolly mammoths became extinct after the last Ice Age, which began around 110,000 years ago and ended around 10,000 years ago.

Woolly mammoths were less well adapted for life on a warmer planet than their cousins, the elephants.

Sometimes change can be more rapid, for example, when a volcano covers a habitat with lava, ash and dust. Rapid changes such as this happen too quickly for animals and plants to adapt, and many individuals die. Many scientists think that dinosaurs became extinct after a meteorite hit Earth and dramatically changed the climate.

Rapid change

It takes many generations for a species to adapt physically to a changing environment. So adaptation happens more quickly in species such as insects, whose life cycles are short. From around 1850 to 1950, there was a lot of soot and other air pollution in the industrial areas of Britain. This made the branches and trunks of trees much darker than before. Light-coloured peppered moths became scarcer than darker moths because they stood out more on the polluted trees and could be spotted easily by bird predators. Developing the darker colour was the peppered moths' adaptation to rapid change. Today, these moths are much lighter again because the air is much cleaner.

Unlike their now-extinct relative, the woolly mammoth, elephants have a tough, leathery skin and no fur. They have adapted to survive in the hot climates of Africa and Asia.

Snow monkeys in Japan have started to frequent hot springs in the last 40 years, moving up cold mountains to escape disturbance by people. They keep warm in the hot water of the springs.

Climate change, or global warming, is now happening very quickly because of human activities. Power plants and vehicles are pumping gases into the atmosphere. These gases store heat and make the world warmer in some areas and wetter or drier in others. No one knows how different animals and plants will adapt to the changing conditions. Scientists think that polar bears may become extinct as they struggle with warming oceans and melting Arctic ice.

CHANGE OF BEHAVIOUR

Animals with longer life cycles can survive rapid environmental changes by adapting their behaviour. For example, a raccoon's natural habitat is the forests of North America. The raccoon is mainly nocturnal and nests in trees, feeding on birds' eggs and other foods. As people cut down more forests, more raccoons are moving to the suburbs. The raccoons use their grasping hands to open dustbins in search of food. Peregrine falcons have adapted to loss of natural habitat by moving into cities to hunt pigeons.

Investigate lichens

Lichens are small, plant-like organisms that live on tree bark or branches or form crusty patches on hard surfaces such as concrete and gravestones. Lichens are special symbiotic organisms. Most of a lichen consists of a spongy or tough fungus. This part shelters lots of algae. Algae make their food by photosynthesis similar to green plants. The algae in lichen also make food for the fungi.

Some lichens are sensitive to air pollution, especially a gas called sulphur dioxide, which is released when factories or vehicles burn fossil fuels. Many lichen species can exist when the air is clean, but only the hardiest, least sensitive types can live in polluted areas. In this activity, your will work in small groups to survey lichens on trees in your local area so you can find out how clean the air is.

GUIDE TO LICHENS

	Fruticose	Foliose	Crustose
Appearance	Branched, plant-like lichens	Like crumbly, dried leaves	Tough, crust-like
Attachment to surfaces	Using a sucker-like holdfast	Attached fairly loosely	Attached firmly
Sensitivity to pollution	Most sensitive	Tolerate some pollution	Least sensitive

You will need:

- notebook and pen
- guide to lichens (see box opposite for a simple guide)
- digital camera (optional)

1. Choose two survey sites where you can safely examine the trees. One should be more polluted than the other. More polluted places include those near to farms or close to traffic (be careful near busy roads). Places with cleaner air include forests, parks and churchyards.

2. Choose three trees of the same type at each site. Identify the lichens on ten small branches. Knowing the species is not as important as recognising the way that they grow. If you are uncertain of the type, take a photo of the twig. (Do not damage or remove the lichens because they grow very slowly and cannot recover quickly.)

3. Estimate the proportion of each type of lichen on each twig. For example, are they all fruticose or are they half fruticose and half crustose (see box)?

4. Add together your data on the proportions of lichen types on each branch and work out the average for each tree at each site. Present your findings as pie charts of lichen types for each tree.

5. Did the types of lichen vary between the survey sites you chose? Do you think your sampling method was fair? How might you improve the survey?

6. Some cities commission lichen surveys every few years to test air quality. Why not go to your local library and see if there have been lichen surveys in your area? Have the lichen types changed over time and, if so, why do you think this has happened?

Glossary

aestivation Passing the summer or dry season in a state of dormancy.

algae Plant-like organisms that do not have leaves, stems, roots or flowers but make food by photosynthesis.

amino acids Basic building blocks of proteins, which organisms need for growth and development.

annuals Plants that grow from seed, reproduce and die in one season or year.

bioluminescence Production of light by living organisms.

biome Distinctive group of ecosystems that covers a large area of the land or water on the Earth's surface. Examples of biomes include deserts or rainforests.

carnivores Animals that eat the flesh of other animals.

conifer Tree adapted to colder climates with needle-like leaves that cover the branches throughout the year.

deciduous Trees that lose their leaves and lie dormant once a year.

dehydrate To dry out.

diurnal Active during the daytime.

dormant Describes an organism at rest, either by hibernation or aestivation. Seeds also lie dormant in times of drought or cold.

echolocation Finding an object by detecting the echoes of sound waves. Bats and dolphins use echolocation to find their way around.

ecosystem All the plants, animals and other living things in a place and the way they interact with each other and their habitat.

epiphytes Plants that grow on other plants for support, often to get themselves into a good position for receiving sunlight.

evaporates/evaporation When a liquid turns into a gas. When clothes dry on a clothes line, the water evaporates into the air.

evolution Process by which every living thing slowly changes over time because of the slight variations in genes from one generation to the next.

fronds Leaf-like parts of ferns and seaweed.

fungi Plant-like organisms that do not contain chlorophyll and so cannot make their own food. Mushrooms, moulds and yeasts are fungi.

germinate/germination When a seed starts to grow.

habitat Place where an organism lives. There are many different habitats in the world, ranging from mountaintops to the ocean depths.

hibernation Passing the winter or cold season in a state of dormancy.

holdfasts Root-like parts of a seaweed that attach the seaweed to the ground. Unlike real roots, holdfasts do not take in water and nutrients.

insulate To slow or block the movement of sound, heat or electricity.

invertebrates Animals that do not have backbones.

larva Stage of growth of some insects after hatching from the egg. Most larvae are wingless and resemble a caterpillar or grub.

migration Movement of animals in search of food or shelter, often in response to seasonal changes.

natural selection Process by which organisms best adapted to their environment tend to outlive and take over from those that are less well adapted.

niche An organism's particular role within its habitat.

nocturnal Active at night.

nutrients Substances that organisms need to live.

organism Any living thing, such as an animal, plant, bacterium or fungus.

parasite Organism that lives on a host organism. The parasite uses the host as a source of food or for protection and may harm, or even kill, it.

pheromone Chemical released by an organism to influence the behaviour of other members of the same species.

photosynthesis Process by which green plants trap energy from sunlight and use it to make food from carbon dioxide and water.

pollen Grains that contain the male reproductive cells of a seed plant.

pollinate To transfer pollen from the flower of one plant to another plant of the same species.

radiation Movement of energy through the air in waves or rays.

reproduce To have offspring.

species A group of organisms that can mate with one another and produce fertile offspring.

symbiosis The mutually beneficial relationship between two different species.

temperate Climate with distinct summer and winter seasons and regular, moderate rainfall.

tissue Collections of cells that work together to do a specific job. Skin cells form skin tissue.

water pressure Downward force of water caused by the pull of gravity.

wetland Low area of land that is saturated (soaked) with water.

Further information

WEBSITES TO VISIT

This website has lots of useful information about evolution and adaptation:
http://evolution.berkeley.edu/evosite/evo101/IIIE5Adaptation.shtml

The BBC Bitesize website contains information on animal adaptations:
www.bbc.co.uk/schools/ks3bitesize/science/biology/adaptation_1.shtml

Investigate adaptation with the fun Dirtmeister science pages at:
http://teacher.scholastic.com/dirtrep/animal/index.htm

Index